MEMORIES
AND MORE

MURRAY DOVAUO

Tellwell Talent
www.tellwell.ca

ISBN
978-0-2288-9557-2 (Hardcover)
978-0-2288-9556-5 (Paperback)
978-0-2288-9558-9 (eBook)

TABLE OF CONTENTS

AND

MORE

ACKNOWLEDGEMENTS

My special thanks to Bonnie, Amy & Karen.
Each has played an essential part,
from the writing to the publication of these poems.

MEMORIES

◇◇◇◇◇◇◇◇◇◇◇◇◇◇◇◇◇◇◇◇◇◇◇◇◇◇◇◇◇◇◇◇◇◇◇◇

The poems in this section are based on times and events of my early years to my present life. While they may seem fanciful there is a true event underlying each poem.

MEMORIES

A world exists beyond my walls
I plainly hear its siren calls
but a deadly virus stalks our land
so in my room, I'll make a stand
I dream of a world that I once knew
of a wide and clear azure sky and golden fields of prairie grain
a little boy playing a lonely game
he has no hero to help him fight
and put those rustlers to hasty flight
his cowboy uncle once rode and wore a gun
but his little games are much more fun
there are grasshoppers and toads that hop about
though he chases them he can never catch
but look? There's a wild and tasty berry patch
but time moves on, a distant future is now today
and his little games he must put away
he's now a part of a remembered past
of childhood days that did not last
but when my life lacks a driving force
nor has it a plan to chart a course
he comes to me and once again we play
those lonely games of yesterday.

***

THE LIGHTS OF HOME

The boy said "I'll go hunting today
upon the mountain a few miles away"
a skiff of snow had fallen there
a little breeze chilled the mountain air
he searched for tracks in the fallen snow
and resting places where a deer might go
there were no signs that he could find
the deer were all in the valley below
time had passed, the hours slipped away
and dusk had come to end the day
he stopped to decide which way he should go
and quickly realized that he did not know
a kind of panic crept into his mind
a fear the way home he may never find
it would be bitterly cold on the mountain top
and with no shelter he dared not stop
he walked on into that lonely night
his companion hope that his way was right
there was no moon to light his way
only darkness that comes to end the day
but suddenly his joy made him cry
just when his hope has almost died
he could see into the valley far below
and there in the distance a welcoming glow
until you have been lost and wandered alone
you'll never know the joy of seeing the lights of home.

***

THE LITTLE HOUSE

The little house stood on land as it used to be
surrounded by fields as far as the eye can see.

The windows were holes in weathered walls
there was no door, just old welcoming halls
patches of wallpaper could still be seen
and bits of wool where carpets had been
parts of the rough board floor had rotted away
to reveal a cellar where food was saved for a rainy day.

And the roof that once gave shelter to those below
no longer repels the assaults of rain and snow
and on the wind rides the prairie dust
covering all in a thick and muddy crust.

As I gazed, a feeling of warmth found me there
and children's voices filled the air
but I knew the warmth was the summer sun
and the voices, just the soft whispering wind.

I walked away for I had far to go
but I'll come again, and this I know
for something in that little house called to me
what it was I did not know, nor could I see.

Was it the echo of a life that once was here
as a reminder of my days, I hold so dear

again I made the journey as I did before
to find the peace I had found once more.

But the little house was gone, leaving not a trace
just ripening fields of grain left in its place
my disappointment was deep, like losing a friend
that little piece of the past had come to its end.

***

THE GOPHER

Thousands of years ago the glaciers withdrew
and left behind a fertile land of grass and slough
and soon into this space nature's creatures came,
they were of many kinds too numerous to name
among them the carnivores that hunt night and day
and the ubiquitous gopher that was their prey
he had no defense nor safety in a surface lair,
so he burrowed into the ground and huddled there
that world existed for many thousand years
then from the east a new enemy now appears
it's a farmer and family with horses and a cow
but most important were his seeds and a plow
he breaks the land, removes the stones and plants the seed
all where the little gopher had his home and used to feed
his home destroyed the little gopher moved to virgin land
but the green shoots of planted seed were close at hand
so he and others raid that farmer's field,
destroying a part of the expected yield
the angry farmer vows he will never rest,
till his land is safe from that little pest
with traps and poisons he wages unending war
and the gopher faces dangers never seen before
in time the farmer is pleased with results obtained
the war is over and a tentative truce is proclaimed
but the beleaguered gopher is not safe yet
for soon to come three little boys and Shep the pet
in the spring they would seek his underground lair,
and with pails of water force him up for air

and when he broke the surface to take a breath,
Shep was waiting there and so was death
that poor little gopher, that little prey and pest
will he ever have a home where he can safely rest?

***

NATURE LOST

Today I went to find a part of my early years
with all its happiness and a few tears.
There was a little house that was home for two
and a little field where only grasses grew.
Where I used to watch the marmots feed and play,
throughout the length of the summer day.
Or lie basking in the rays of a noon day sun
'til a hungry coyote came and spoiled their fun.
And sometimes during a long summer day
a circling hawk watched for its furry prey.
But when the evening shadows were growing long
from time to time a grazing stag would appear
or perhaps it would be two or three graceful deer
and when night had fallen and all was still,
I could hear a truck climb a faraway hill.
Or that haunting whistle of a moving train
that lonesome sound can touch your very soul
and make you glad that you are not alone.
In the distance a mountain towers up in the air
and by the rivers bend a little city nestles there.
But reality intrudes as it always must
and dreams of yesterday return to dust.
The little house looks the same as when it was mine,
but the field has been lost to the wants of a newer time
covered by homes where once the marmots played.
It's sad to see the loss of a piece of an earlier day.
For the little field had lived as nature planned,
and the laws of nature were in command.

***

A COUNTRY ROAD

My mind went back to my childhood days
and I relived my childish ways.
The prairie hills I know so well, I clearly see
and with the little road, they're a special part of me.

I travelled that little road on my trusty steed
and none could match her blazing speed.
My deadly sword was always by my side
and where I rode, all would step aside.

Of the beasts and dragons that stalked the land
I slew them all with my deadly sword in my hand
but time is the enemy of childish ways
for it makes the past of childhood days.

My pretend road fades as I look back
and is again a simple country track
it climbs each hill and crosses each dell
and skirts each slough where ducks may dwell.

When I looked to where it meets the skies
I knew somewhere out there my future lies
and I knew no matter how far I roam
that little road will call and take me home.

***

THE COW AND THE CAT

A neighbour was moving far away
the farm was sold they leave today
the lady asked, could she leave her cat?
The answer was yes and that was that
soon the cat felt right at home
from house to barn it would roam
but cats are smart they quickly see
where milking is done is the place to be
they wait for a squirt of nice warm milk
and feel it in their throat as smooth as silk
in the spring on an early sunny morn
a little brown calf was newly born
she is yours the father told his son
but be sure your other chores are all done
how that boy loved that little brown calf
to see it run and jump made him laugh
when in the barn she ignored mice and rats
but for some unknown reason she hated cats
the little calf was now a cow
she was to be milked, the boy knew how
on the morning of that memorable day
he took his stool and pail to where she lay
she wasn't tied for she wouldn't run
in a few minutes the job would be done
he didn't see the cat there for its treat
in a flash, he was knocked from his seat
he looked around from where he lay
there was a sight you don't see every day

the cat was running to escape a charging brute
the cow, well she was there in hot pursuit
the cat survived, I am not sure how
the boy cried
"Someone else milk that stupid cow."

***

DIMPLES

Dimples was a little white pony whose ears were brown
she was born in the prairie hills far from town
the love of a child was all she knew
a love she returned both gentle and true
she never knew the sting of an angry quirt
nor the painful jab of an impatient spur
she never tried to herd a wily old cow
nor know the tiring labour of pulling a plow
with a little girl she roamed the hills on summer days
those prairie hills where herds of buffalo used to graze
but the passing years ended that idealistic life
for that little girl was now a woman and a wife
and soon children took her place at Dimples' side
where they played their little games and learned to ride
Dimples never reacted to the childish laughter and cries
she just watched with her gentle and questioning eyes
with a child she again roamed the prairie hills
just as she had in those happy days years before
there was a depression and the land was dry
life was hard no matter how hard one may try
the family decided they would have to move away
but Dimples was old and would have to stay
left behind the family wondered where she could go
and they worried for they did not know
but a family that knew Dimples came to say
they would give her a home where she could stay

as she left it was hard to hold back the tears
for she had been a pet all through her years
but Dimples was happy, her life complete
for it ended with love just like it began.

***

MY WORLD

From my window I can clearly see
a world that once belonged to me
it was my world, I played my part
its familiar ways were close to my heart
there were rivers and little streams
and lakes of which an artist dreams
trees climb the mountains to meet the snow
that in the moonlight has a magic glow
fields of grain stretch as far as I can see
that in the fall became a golden sea
the land is dotted with cities and little towns
and roads that take me wherever I wished to go
like the eagle that flies high above
I could fly and see my world far below
but time is a thief that stole my years
now my world has become a memory
as I gaze out my window there I see
a world I don't know, it doesn't belong to me.

***

A WINTER NIGHT

Winter has come to the prairie hills
summers warmth replaced by bitter chills
a coat of snow covers the frozen ground
that seems to dampen every sound
in the sky each star a twinkling light
and a moon that creates a magical night
there is no wind to moan around the eaves
or sway the limbs of the barren trees
and all the creatures that own the night
are silent shadows in the brilliant moonlight
an expectant hush falls over the land
as if waiting for a ghostly image to appear
there is a stillness in the arctic air
that touches the soul of anyone there
you stand transfixed in silence and awe
by a magical picture only nature could draw.

***

A SPRING DAY

Spring has come to the prairie hills
its warmth replacing those winter chills
there is a coat of green instead of snow
the land is alive with a beauty we know
the sky is an unbroken canopy of heavenly blue
the sun a ship on that sea of heavenly hue
a gentle breeze whispers around the eaves
and little birds twitter among the trees
timid gophers cower in an underground lair
wary of a hawk circling high in the air
there is an energy that comes from the land
and a confidence for its all in natures hand
the joyous sounds of spring fill the air
the silence of winter is no longer there
while artists may draw the world that they see
they can't match the picture nature can be.

***

A SUMMER DAY

Summer has come to the prairie hills
under the midday sun all is still
the fields are green with sprouting grain
the earth is waiting for that needed rain
but there were no clouds to hide the sun
that bakes the land till day is done
in the distance heat waves ripple in the air
and little creatures seek cover in a cooling lair
the only shade is there under the trees
where animals gather neath the leaves
there is a lethargy that touches all things
the herds that graze and the birds that sing
it saps the energy to do what must be done
and brings a sleepy feeling to everyone
artists may paint the sunshine on a prairie hill
but to include emotions requires natures skill.

***

AN AUTUMN DAY

Autumn has come to the prairie hills
between summer heat and winter chills
fields of stubble lay basking in the midday sun
the harvest is over summer work is done
there is a calmness to each autumn day
as the long days of summer fade away
the trees somehow know now is the time
to paint the land in colours sublime
all the creatures prepare for bitter days
each one following their own unique ways
some to sleep when the nights are long
others to spread their wings and follow the sun
there is a kind of contentment in the air
the stress of summer no longer there
while an artist may paint beautiful leaves
only nature can add that gentle breeze.

***

THE LITTLE BEAR

The little bear was curled up in its wire pen
alone far from its mother's cozy den
it was tiny it needed a mother's care
no matter how it cried she wasn't there
it's mother no doubt had met her end
it would never know her love ever again
it would never live a life of free will
it would never explore a forested hill
it would never climb those old dead trees
to steal the honey from the angry bees
it would never find ants in a rotten log
or search for food in a wet land bog
it would never hunt marmots in a scree
or catch migrating fish in a gurgling stream
it need not find a den at summers end
for it would never be free ever again
every little whimper tore at my heart
tho in its care I played no part
I couldn't just stand idly by
I must do something I had to try
I reached in and gently stroked its ear
and at my touch it tried to nestle near
as I stroked the whimpers gradually eased
that tiny little bear was sound asleep

***

STARS

We have many friends as years go by
each like a star in the evening sky
to have many friends is a precious thing
your world is one of eternal spring
my sky was filled with twinkling lights
like a cloudless sky on a winter's night.

In my younger days there were no tears
for I was living my carefree years
but those middle years so far away
no longer the future, they're now today
rarely does a new star appear
I am content with old friends so dear.

But time is never still, it marches on
and my middle years now are gone
my stars begin to die, leaving empty space
and darkness comes to take their place
my stars no longer shine as once they did
and loneliness resides where they once lived.

But a new star has appeared in my sky
brighter than any in the years gone by
it's a new and caring friend
in whose warmth my heart will mend.

***

GOLDEN YEARS

My wife met me at our door
something she had never done before
I showed her the watch I got that day
and told her the words they had to say
she held me close there were no fears
for we were entering our golden years
now be it work or be it pleasure
whatever we do we'll do together
we stayed in our old familiar home
but we were often away, we loved to roam
then an autumn chill would touch the air
and we could no longer linger there
we were excited a new adventure had begun
and like the honking goose we'll follow the sun
winters were spent in a land of tropical breeze
and of sand washed by southern seas
we had no tasks to fill our days
we found contentment in our idle ways
the years passed quickly or so it seemed
now they exist only as lovely dreams
but time also took our vagabond ways
and brought us to life's autumn days
when evening comes and brings a stillness to the land
I go to her and softly take her wrinkled hand
And still together we relive those golden years.

***

AND

◇◇◇◇◇◇◇◇◇◇◇◇◇◇◇◇◇◇◇◇◇◇◇◇◇◇◇◇◇◇◇◇◇◇◇◇◇◇◇

These poems are the first that were written. They were written soon after the pandemic was declared, and represent the high regard I have for the home staff.

CHOICES

At last you've come to a senior's home
a place where you're no longer alone
but you ask "What does it do for me?"
This is a new life what will it be?"
But you don't need to feel any despair
for its run by love and tender care
you can still do things you did before
like visit old friends or go to the store
you can travel or stay at home with a book
you will find games to play when you look
the people here are just like you
to find an easier life where tasks are few
but most of all there will be friends
just make a few and loneliness ends.

***

HOME

My years are many, my strength is gone
I know it's not safe for me to live alone
so I have left a place I once called home
from whose shelter I swore I would never roam
a place where a little family used to live
a place with all the happiness love could give
now my life is not like the one I lived before
where I could shut out the world with my door
in this life there are games or events for each day
so I can fill my hours in my own chosen way
but there's a caring staff that tends to me
they do all the little chores and set me free
but how can they make this into a home
when it's full of strangers I'll never know
it's a daily challenge the staff must face
and it must be met with love and grace
they do it all with a smile and tenderness
they are special people we should daily bless.

***

THE MIND

There was a yearning in my room today
a yearning that took my breath away
it's something I could sense in my mind
it searched for a challenge it couldn't find
my familiar puzzles won't fill the need
nor was it something I could read
I could go to the Bistro and find a chair
beside someone who is already there
we can talk of the weather as acquaintances do
or talk of the life we each once knew
but however long this life of mine may last
its sorrows belong in the distant past
the answer I seek must be in my room
perhaps it is there in the evening gloom
I wonder if I could write a poem
a poem of life and love as it should be
a poem that tells of sadness and of strife
a poem that tells of an unhappy life
as my mind sought words that belong
I find the yearning is replaced by song
as I review the day one thing is clear
do not restrict the mind to the near and dear
let it live in a world of hopes and dreams
let it imagine weird plans and crazy schemes
you may say it's too old and slow
but it can be happy just make it so.

***

SPECIAL ANGELS

A fear has swept across the peaceful land
we pause and try to understand
it's a plague! We hear the cry
and some of us will surely die
but wiser heads rise up and give us rules
to help us fight this long deadly duel
but I'm in a home, what can I do?
Then from our midst our special angels appear
they guard our lives and risk their own
so now I'm safe within their care
now I can think of future times
when we grumble, as we are prone to do
when in our minds we forget
in our hearts an abiding love exists
for those special angels in our midst.

***

A PRINCESS

A princess has royalty to set her apart
but I say it's someone with a caring heart
someone who cares for the crippled and old
someone whose love never grows cold
who accepts the stress of many long hours
and is always there for someone in need.
There is a home where seniors reside
with a caring aide never far from their side
each aide is a princess in my mind
a more caring staff you may never find
everyone has shown a loving heart
everyone is willing to do their part
as an example, there's one everyone knows
it's Liana, a princess wherever she goes.

***

THE GENTLE WARRIOR

An invisible dragon attacks our shores
and where it passes leaves behind
a deadly virus we've never seen before
we have no weapons, what can we do
but as before when panic reigns
a guide comes forward and takes the reins
her smile is gentle, her voice is soft
but her resolve is made of steel
she bears a confidence we can feel
she has no guns or rumbling tanks of war
she has only science and common sense.
She comes before us every day
she takes our hand and leads the way
the way will be hard, it will be long
but with her help we will be strong
but with passing time our will does sag
we grow weary, our spirits flag
that gentle voice again is heard
it lifts our spirits to carry on
some will falter, some will fall
but with her help, we'll all stand tall
our gentle warrior – Dr. Bonnie Henry.

***

LISA

The life we shared with you will end today
to a new one you will go and with the old one we will stay.
With heavy hearts we wish you success and happiness with no end
for you are more to us than just a friend.
And should adversity ever test your will
we hope our wishes will ease your climb up every hill.
For now, we want you to know
how grateful we are that you were here.
For when an evil came that had no cure
you faced the enemy and never wavered in our defense.
We owe you a debt we can never pay
so we'll hold you in our hearts and there you'll stay.
But now we say goodbye with a smile and in its shadow our tears
will hide.
Adios amigo, go in peace with our love forever by your side.

***

OUR ANGEL

The story is that all the angels are in heaven
if so, then there is a heaven here on earth
for one has come to travel with us on our chosen road
and spend time with us in our senior's abode
she has no wings so she might hover in the air
nor a halo you can see but you know it's there
she lives a life that matches ours in every way
and shows the love she has for us every day
she pushes her drink cart along every aisle
and greets each one with a word and a smile
should anyone feel the pangs of loneliness
go to her and they will find they are not alone.
But should anyone doubt she is an angel in disguise
then see the compassion in her pretty brown eyes.
Should anyone ask who it is this angel may be
she is there before us for all to see
her name's Diana.

***

THE GALLANT WARRIORS

A virus attacks us from every side, it's everywhere there's no place
   to hide,
We have no weapons to fight this war, it's an enemy we've never
   seen before.

With courage our gallant warriors face the foe, and if it was within
   their powers to give,
every one of us would surely live, they know that most of us will
   survive,
and despite their efforts too many will die.

They formulate rules and all they ask, is that we keep our distance
   and wear a mask,
sanitize our hands whatever we do and keep our contacts to
   very few,
if we obey these rules as fully as we can, it will slow the virus'
   advance across the land.

Unfortunately, there is a thoughtless selfish few, who cry out "I'm
   not afraid I'm immune"
and with no mask they crowd into a tiny space,
despite being told it's a very dangerous place
for they don't know or don't care, that the deadly virus is also
   there.

Now because of a few with no common sense, many are put at risk
   and have no defense
our courageous warriors watch with dismay,
we see the results of their efforts swept away.

With tired bodies and heavy hearts, they carry on, for despite their
      distress all hope is not gone
they know that a vaccine will come at last, and this evil foe will
      only exist in the past.

How do you thank them for all they've done?
You could strike a medal for each and every one
but with time medals go into a drawer, and people will ask "What
      was that for?"
Perhaps a coin or a stamp would do
or maybe a plaque to hang on the wall
but however, we decide to express our thanks
it must have meaning down through they years.

***

MY DAY

The rising sun has found me where I rest
it's warm and comforting in my cozy nest
but in my bed I can no longer stay
the dawn has heralded the start of another day
I look in the mirror. What is that I can see?
Can that old and wrinkled face be really me
but that is silly of course it is I must know
its just that ninety plus years are starting to show
now I am up, there are a number of things I must do
I'll get started as soon as I find my other shoe
I have toast and coffee and make my bed
then try to find a book I have not read
the library is stocked with puzzles and books galore
there must be hundreds and then some more
there is a section that's called romance
Will I ever go there? Not a chance.
What I want is cops and sneaky spies
and bombs raining down out of the skies
now it's time to go and ride the bike
or to go outside and take a hike
but at last lunch time is finally here
I don't suppose there'll be any beer
I don't want to sound crabby or gruff
but I hope there's none of that foreign stuff
then I'll go to my room and read my book
and think how inviting the bed does look
the day moves, it's time for a coffee break
and whatever the cook decided: cookies or cake

now I could gossip and tell some lies
about how hard life was and how time flies
but I'd rather do puzzles to tax my mind
jigsaw or crossword I don't care, either kind
one thing I would like to know, it's no crime
why do they call it dinner when it is supper time?
But it doesn't matter I don't really care
I imagine it's just someone putting on airs
I look at the menu and I think oh boy!
Who ever heard of a vegetable called Bok Choy
now my day is done at last
now one would ever say it was a blast
but no matter how old and bent I may be
the lovely management and staff are a joy to see.

***

MORE

These works are not based on personal experiences, rather they come from personal observations and thoughts I've had throughout my long life.

FATE

I worry not what the future holds for me
my thoughts are of a life that used to be
of the day when my love became my bride
and vowed forever to be by my side.

She was the rock on which I built my dreams
she gave me the courage to spread my wings
I see the struggle during those early years
though times were hard, there were no tears.

The years rushed by; we had done our best
our work was done, now we could rest
but plans made by man are not set in stone
and fate decreed I must go on alone.

My days are full of books and friends who care
but by night my loneliness is waiting there
in my lonely bed I dream of those happy years
and of the unwavering love she gave to me.

As I dream, I reach to hold her close
but she is not here, I am alone
with aching heart, I remember her words to me
out beyond the stars, there I will be.

***

CRY

You came to me and asked "why do you cry?"
With eyes filled with tears, I replied

I cry for the mother who has lost her son
in some war a megalomaniac has begun

and for the child left all on its own
who will never know the love of a parental home

I cry for the victim of family abuse
where violence flares at every excuse

and for the handicapped with their limited way
who will never know the joy of running and play

I cry for the addicts and the life they know
for that euphoric feeling, they give up their soul

and for the poor, and the life they live
and their dreams of the pleasure this world can give

I cry for the old who must live in a home
whose family and friends have gone on before

and for all those who suffer in various ways
and I cry for myself and my lonely ways.

***

HALCYON

The world is full of sadness and despair
she desperately needs our help and loving care
so where is the joy of living and happiness
instead of this life of tension and stress
there is a place I go and there I always find
it eases the pressure I feel and clears my mind
it's a place high on a mountain just below the trees
a place caressed by a gentle mountain breeze
the silence is broken by the scream of a hawk
and by the whistle of a marmot that sees me there
but the sounds are not alien for here they belong
they have beauty they're a part of natures song
there is no loneliness though I am alone
here in this place, I feel this is my home
there is no clock to show the hours clicking by
just the sun sailing across an azure sky
so I ask is this how man was meant to live
I don't know I have no answer I can give
my minds at peace the stress is gone
the sun tells me the day is done I must go
but there is one thing with certainty I know
to this halcyon place I'll come again.

***

TIDES OF LIFE

The life into which we all will grow
is like the tides that ebb and flow
while gentle waves caress the shore
we care not that to life there is more
but the rising tide is very strong
we find our innocent ways do not belong
so with the tide beneath our feet
we rise to see a world we've yet to meet
its siren call is loud and clear
we must leave this life we hold so dear
we enter a world of joys and strife
and in its shadow, we build a life
some have goals for which they strain
more accept the future's loss or gain
but the tide must turn, it cannot last
and the life we know is now our past
some will cling to a life with familiar ways
while others enjoy their autumn days
but it matters not by which road we go
we cannot stem the ebbing flow.

***

BEAUTY

Our world has beauty if you but stop and look
you will see it there in the little babbling brook
or that little bird that greets the spring
and from a bough you hear it sing
in the rose that opens wide its welcoming arms
to lure the fluttering butterfly with all its charms
the magnificent stag that poses in the evening dusk
or the far-off mountain with its crown of snow
in the light of a silvery moon see how it glows
but beauty goes beyond this world of ours
you see it there in the midnight stars
but there is another beauty we know is there
for it describes the love of those who really care
the ones with gentle hands care for the old
the ones who teach the little ones how to live
the ones who say those magic words "I forgive"
the stranger who reaches out a helping hand
and those who risk their lives, to protect our land
there are many more, I can't name them all
but when there is a need they answer the call
so open your eyes to the beauty that is everywhere
just imagine how stark our world would be if it wasn't there.

***

THE HUNT

Large flakes of snow floated down
the trees all wore a snowy crown
all was still, the snow lay deep
in the forest an old stag lay asleep.
An old hunter smiles because he knows
deer are helpless in the deeper snow
they all lay quiet, they do not roam
he would go and bring a trophy home
the stag awakens, he had naught to fear
till from the trees the hunter appears
with a bound to his feet, the stag was gone
the hunter smiles, the hunt would not be long
the stag floundered; he did his best
but more and more often he had to rest
and when he stopped to get some air
it seemed the hunter was always there
one more time the stag rose to his feet
he crossed a meadow then into the trees
this was the end he knew he could not run
now he waited for the hunter and his gun
the hunter thought of the struggle thru the snow
how the stag came so far, he didn't know
he was tired and now a long way from home
he could not take his trophy so far alone
with a sigh he turned and walked away
there'd be another hunt another day
the forest was still the snow lay deep
in the trees an old stag lay fast asleep.

***

44

LIFE'S PHASES

Life has no continuous flow
it has phases we enter as we grow
with our birth our journey begins.

Phase one has lessons on how to live
lessons on when to take and when to give
those lessons are there in children's play
and at school and home every day
finally, your lessons are done you stand alone
and you enter a life that is now your own.

In this phase you choose the life you will live
will that choice be one of take or one of give
will you be a friend to those you know
or will you be shunned wherever you go
but this phase will end no matter what you do
and a new one begins, and days of rest come to you.

You have earned your place in the setting sun
now you are at ease, your race is run
now there's time for those things you longed to do
with your love you can have a life just for two
you can be together just holding hands
there are no words, your contentment says it all.

***

WOMAN

In mythical Greece women did not exist
I don't know if they were ever missed
then Zeus the god grew angry with man
for accepting gifts that Zeus had banned
but man was desperate to improve his life
a life of despair and overwhelming strife
Zeus decided man must dearly pay
and forever in an emotional way
the thought of a woman came to his mind
so he created one, the very first of her kind
no one had ever seen such beauty before
but her beauty was just a pretty facade
for Zeus had given her a cold, cold heart
she was his revenge, she would do her part
I wondered if it was still true today
I'll think about it before I can say
I think of a few women I know today
and tried to imagine the part they play
they are all beautiful with loving hearts
but are they still playing their historic parts
I'm just a simple man, how would I know
for with a smile, they can make anything so
my instinct said they are what they seem
beautiful women of who men dream
there's an old saying I believe is true
"Chase a pretty woman until she catches you."

***

THE DREAM

The old man dozes off in his rocking chair
and a familiar dream comes to him there
he dreams man has a home among the stars
and the land of their birth is left far behind
the dream is of a world as it should be
a world he knows he will never see
he dreams mother nature will play her part
to restore the land guided by a loving heart
once again, the air is pure the waters clean
and the hills are dressed in coats of evergreen
in the valley leafy trees offer shade in summertime
and in the fall paint the land in colours sublime
the prairie grasses grow and ripen in the sun
and feeding animals have no fear of man's deadly gun
the lofty peaks wear a crown of pure white snow
that feed the meandering rivers far below
rivers that flow into a pristine sea
that teems with the life that used to be
there are no wars with death and cruelty hand in hand
nor inquisitive man to once again abuse the land
the old man awakens and sees the world of today
and as dreams do his familiar dream fades away
but he believes he saw the future as it will be
when the dream world he saw becomes reality.

***

THE MOUNTAIN

A massive mountain loomed over the valley below
its summit reaching for heaven, capped with snow
no trees grew to hide its forbidding face
huge boulders were scattered around its base
centuries pass before we see the valley once more
and find huge boulders covering its grassy floor
there is a hill by its side where trees now grow
they tremble and sway when the west winds blow
massive stones lie half buried among the leaves
there is a legend of a mountain that no one believes
a mountain so huge it reached so high
a pillar so strong it must hold up the sky
surely it must have been a sacred place
to help defeat all dangers people must face
there is a lesson to learn from that legend of old
even the sun that burns so bright will grow cold.

***

THE STORM

The quiet land lay dusty and dry
the sun hung in a pale blue sky
the clouds were woolly and white
the day was both still and bright
in the distance a dark line does appear
and with passing time it draws near
a breeze began to shake the trees
and whistle a tune around the eaves
the storm struck with a pounding rush
and soon the dry land was all awash
water flowed down every hill
and every hollow began to fill
in a few moments the storm was gone
but the gift it gave will linger on
the land now sparkles where it lay
the air a cool drink on a summery day
though filled with fury it brought the rain
the earth needs such storms to come again.

***

LIFE STAGES

An old friend came to see me yesterday
I found interest in what he had to say
he spoke of his family, they're doing well
the pride that he feels you could easily tell.

He spoke of old friends and of times we knew
and how the passing of time has left so few
he mentioned how our town seemed to grow
he said it's not the one we used to know.

The things he spoke of, in my mind I could see
and a remembered pleasure they brought to me
but that pleasure soon would pass away
and I thought of the life I'm living today.

I need no plan to meet a future that will be
There is just today's fleeting hours that I see
but the human mind is never at rest
so with no future, it will review the past.

Visions will appear before my eyes
scenes of happy days or of troubled skies
scenes from youth and impossible schemes
or of a family and love to fill my dreams.

But whatever memory the mind may choose
it's wrapped in loneliness it will never lose.

***

ABOUT THE AUTHOR

The author spent his childhood in the province of Saskatchewan, where he developed a love for nature. The following years were spent in British Columbia. He now resides in a seniors' home in Kamloops. He discovered his poetic talent in his mid 90's during the pandemic. His poems reflect his wisdom, humor and compassion for the world.